LEARN ABOUT PAGANISM

Ostara

WITH

Grani Hulda

Pagan Books for Pagan Kids

Grani Hulda

This book
belongs to:

_____

What is Ostara?

Ostara is a holy day celebrated by Pagans around the world. It is celebrated at the Spring Equinox.

At Ostara, night and day are the same lengths. The light and dark are balanced.

This balance happens twice each year. It happens once at the Spring Equinox and once at the Fall Equinox.

Spring is the time of year when the Sun starts gaining power and the Earth comes alive.

The Greening Begins

Because there is more light, the grass is growing. Trees are starting to get leaves, and flowers are coming up.

Birds are singing and building nests.

Grani Hulda is starting to plant her garden.

Butterflies, bees and caterpillars are out in the sun.

A lot of baby animals are born during Ostara season. It is a time of birth and renewal.

The Ostara Tale

The Goddess Ostara turned a bird into a hare. The hare thanked her by laying colored eggs at her festival every year after that.

Hares are very fertile and have a lot of babies. That's why there are so many eggs.

Every year the Ostara Hare brings us colored eggs to celebrate Spring.

Celebrate Ostara

There are many ways to celebrate Ostara.

Ostara is a good time to make wands and good luck charms for your home, like Ostara wreaths and pentacles.

An altar is a good way to tell the Goddess Ostara "Thank You" for all the blessings that we receive.

You can make Ostara gift baskets for people that you love to show them that you appreciate them.

Enjoy all the signs of Spring.

Hunting for eggs is a fun way to celebrate Ostara.

Fires and dancing are ways to celebrate Ostara. These are often done with friends, but you can do them by yourself, too.

Ostara celebrations and festivals are ways that we can show our love for our planet.

Printed in Great Britain
by Amazon